We Do Not Know Ourselves,
We Discover Ourselves.....

FOOTSTEPS TO WISDOM PUBLISHING

Other books by Jean-Jacques Trifault:

Everything is a Gift
God is in My Heart
Gratitude to the Creation
An Open Heart Comes from an Open Mind
Can We Be the Gift for Someone?
How to Live Life
Among Those Born of Women There was None Greater Than John
The Body of Christ
The Rebirth of God and Lisa
(Several books are translated into French and Spanish.)

To order books, please visit the author's website:
www.footstepstowisdom.org

ISBN: 978-0-9847433-2-2

Cover design and book layout by Kasia Krawczyk

We Do Not Know Ourselves,
We Discover Ourselves.....

When people are seated at a café table waiting for their order to arrive, they have a tendency to look around at people at other tables, and even make comments about them, saying in discreet voices, "I think he looks like this kind of person…." Or, "I think she must be like that…." Interestingly, while one person might offer a certain explanation, someone else could bring a totally different view, saying, "No, I don't think he is like that, I think he is like this….."

Seeing this situation we could question, can what people observe be that much different? Or, is each person just looking from a different angle? Finally, if they were to tell the person at the other table what they concluded about him, he would probably respond, "I really don't think I'm like that!"

Based on these conflicting viewpoints, we can say that we all see from different perspectives. As well, if we ask all the people at the café who they think they are, they may seem hesitant when it comes to describing their characters.

Can we therefore conclude that people are often confused about who they think they are? Many times when people say something about themselves, what they are describing at that moment and what they said a week ago does not seem like the same person. What happened? Based on the different ways they describe themselves, we could believe they are trying to discover who they are, which might be the reason their views keep changing.

Regardless of the complexity of human beings, are there some things that we do know about ourselves? As a start, we can say we are women or men, if we observe the shapes of our bodies. But regardless of this envelope called 'male' or 'female', is there more that we want to know about ourselves? How about all the magazines for women out there? There are so many. Surely the idea behind these magazines is to help the woman who tries to find herself. And, what about men? Does their section in the magazine rack express what a man is?

Observing the huge mass of literature that is created for the purpose of helping us discover ourselves, we might offer the comment that our Creator must be very smart to be able to make us in such a way that we can never find out completely who we are! What if God created us in such a way that we could discover who we are in just a few short years? Surely, if we were able to find out who we are so easily, we would have a greater chance of becoming bored during our lifetime.

Regardless of how we were originally made, one thing is sure: today we find ourselves trying to analyze who we are. This is the reason we can often hear our-

selves remark, "I think I'm like this…" or "I think I'm not like this…" As well, due to our desire to have an absolute understanding of who we are, if someone tells us something different from our view of ourselves, we may have a hard time to believe it.

Yet, if we observe how life unfolds around us, we will realize everything moves and changes, passing through different stages. A plant, for example, starts as a seed and progresses to a stage of stems and leaves in order to be able to eventually create flowers and fruits.

The Effect of Making a Statement

Humans also must pass through different stages of evolution and as a result of this development we can say that we cannot be persons who stay the same, but rather we are persons who never stay the same. Due to the many situations that demand our interaction with them, we have the honor to change over and over, discovering who we are on the way.

We are on Earth in order to discover ourselves.

If we can accept this idea of discovering ourselves, instead of believing 'I know who I am', then we will have a better viewpoint towards life. To "know" ourselves is like drawing a square around ourselves: what is inside the square defines what we are, and what is outside does not belong to us. But if we choose the viewpoint that we are on Earth in order to discover ourselves, we will be more open to discovering new desires or interests inside us. This means there will be no end, no limitation to expanding ourselves.

Of course, it requires time and effort to become what

we desire to be. However, if we often find ourselves using the phrase, "I know who I am" or "I think this is who I am," we will never have a chance to evolve. Instead we will object to many situations: "I think I am not made for this….I think I cannot do that." Based on making this kind of statement over and over, we will mold our characters in such a way that produces a stronger sense of who we are, to the point we will firmly state, "I know who I am."

At this stage we are boxed in, and if some situation requires that we make changes, we will say, "I cannot accept this situation because it's not me." Even if we are friends with someone who pushes us to do something that we believe is not in our character, we will say to our friend, "It is a nice idea, but don't try to convince me because I will not do it. Remember, I know what I like."

The problem of making too many statements about who we are is that our perspective on life is hindered, making it nearly impossible to check if our life is improving or deteriorating. The statement of belief, 'I know who I am', will blind us to many opportunities that arise or to something that needs to be adjusted in ourselves. More dangerously, this kind of statement will make us incapable of sensing our internal direction.

What is interesting about these 'inoffensive' words that sound so convincing, is that when we begin to repeat to ourselves, 'I know who I am," we will find ourselves rejecting any ideas presented by our partner, family or friends. Based on the belief that we know ourselves, it will not be surprising to find ourselves saying, "I think I won't like this…or that…or this."

Due to our perpetual rejection of new ideas, anyone who tries to approach us and experiences rejection over and over will also have the opportunity to create a concept of who we are. Unfortunately, this person's view toward us might be so different from our own viewpoint that these two views can collide. Eventually, this person might even confront us with the accusation that we are basically always negative or protecting ourselves from change.

Unfortunately, a person who believes he knows who he is will usually find a way to reject someone who offers him an opportunity to change. For example, if we approach this kind of person with an idea to go hiking in the mountains, he might reply to us, "I don't think I have the right body type for hiking, and anyway, I am more of a city person." Basically, this answer means that we will not have anyone to go hiking with in the mountains that weekend.

If some people believe they are city people, there is an opposite situation where people believe they are only countryside people, not made for the city. If we say to the one who believes he needs to be in the countryside, "I think you might enjoy living in the city," surely we will hear from him the reflection, "Really, me?"

By making the statement, 'I know who I am', we will often find ourselves rejecting people's ideas and any opportunities that present themselves to us. Basically, due to this wonderful concept of believing we know ourselves, we end up erecting so many walls around us that it is impossible to welcome any new idea. We will find ourselves becoming more rigid as we age, which can as well lead to different emotional and health problems.

Despite these negative consequences, people usually work hard to ensure that their character never changes. For example, if we return to our hometown, we will realize that many of our former acquaintances behave similarly to when they were younger, just with older bodies. Indeed, seeing the contrast of older bodies with the same characteristics can be alarming!

Regardless we might believe it is good to know who we are, this will cause us to reject many new possibilities.

So, regardless we might believe it is good to know who we are, this will cause us to reject many new possibilities, developing ever more sophisticated justifications and objections to protect our view of ourselves. Some rejections can do more damage to us than others. For example, we might begin to say, "I think I am not meant to be a mother." Indeed, we can observe in this time that there are a lot of young women who struggle about marriage and motherhood. The pity is that these women have a tendency to believe that it is really impossible to be a mother. And, regardless a woman might jump into a marriage and find herself having a child, she might still maintain the thought that she is not made to have a family. Due to this conflict, where on the one hand she has a family and on the other hand she feels it is not in her character to be a mother, she can come to the point where she cannot make it any more.

We Create Based on Who We Are

The reason we try so hard to define ourselves is because of a fear of not finding ourselves. However, when we begin to think we know who we are, we end up squeezing ourselves into a small space where we can no longer breathe. If God tries to approach people like this, saying, "You can be perfect" it is understandable why they could reply, "Me, perfect? I cannot be perfect. Look, I am this or that…" In other words, they are already convinced that they cannot become perfect.

Basically, we have a tendency to reject any new idea because we are focused upon what we are in the present time. When we say we know ourselves, often we are choosing a specific point that we like about ourselves and rejecting everything else.

So now, do you want to know who you are? The best answer will be that I do not want to know myself, but I want to accept to discover what I am made of. By choosing the approach that we are on Earth to discover ourselves, we will be able to welcome many different situations that people will offer us, and the events we encounter will enrich our characters, step-by-step.

If we look at history, we can discern people's view of themselves by looking at what they created. For example, in the Middle, or Dark Ages, people must have had the view that life was just a battle for survival, to the point that what they created around them corresponded exactly to their viewpoint. Since the towns of the Middle Ages were built with thick walls, surely we can surmise that the people must have built great walls within themselves. And, if we have a chance to enter a fortress or a castle built during this period, we will realize the rooms inside are small and dark, demonstrating that the people also had created narrow, dark spaces within themselves.

If we believe what people create demonstrates who they are, then if we meet a person who creates a lot of physical protection around himself, we know it will be difficult to break the walls of his character. Likewise, if some people in the Middle Ages wanted to end the time when the castle-fort was the national identity, they needed to find a way to change people's viewpoints or characters. Therefore, regardless it was a good idea to end this kind of defensive identity, we know that many people who wanted change had to lose their lives fighting against the ones who considered that things should stay the way they were.

Regardless many fortresses were eventually destroyed and only a few remain, have people really destroyed the walls of their characters, or do they continue to try to solidify their thoughts in order to maintain that they 'know' who they are? If today human beings continue to build their personal 'fortresses' through insisting they know themselves, this situation can be viewed as a sort of modern 'Dark Ages'.

Do you wonder whether God could visit human beings during the time of the Dark Ages? Surely we can guess that God must have wanted to run as far away from people as perhaps they themselves wanted to flee from those fearful fortresses. And, regardless it is not specified why people call that time period 'the Dark Ages', if we consider God as being the Light, then it is understandable why this era of history was called what it was.

Based on this historical reality, if human beings persist in believing they know who they are, this will continue to create walls so thick that the energy of God can barely pass through. And sadly, due to the lack of energy or light, people will not even perceive they are living in their own private 'Dark Ages'.

Therefore, to avoid creating massive walls, it is best to begin the journey towards our destiny by saying, "I am

living every single day to discover something in myself."
With this thought we can expand our borders instead of
walling ourselves in.

When We Change, Our Relationships Change

When we meet someone, we first usually try to check out
his or her character, and if we like what we see, we might
feel the desire to become friends with this person, and
eventually create a deeper, more permanent relationship
with him or her. Basically, people try to marry with someone who has characteristics that please them.

But, if after a few years of marriage they no longer see what they had
seen in the beginning, and if they insist on finding the same characteristics
in their partner, then that marriage
will fall apart because their partner has
changed. The reality is that regardless
people believe they know themselves or
know their partners, life slowly changes
everyone, sooner or later.

Regardless people believe they know themselves or know their partners, life slowly changes everyone.

Still, regardless that life remodels
people, the question is, how will each
partner cope with change in the other partner? Will one
reject what the other has become because this is not the
person he or she married? If a husband confronts his wife,
"You have changed," she may respond, "Of course I am
changing, what do you think?" And maybe he will coun-
ter, "But you were like this when I married you, and now
you are different."

We might wonder, did he marry her with the acceptance that life could influence her, or did he marry her with the idea that nothing should ever change in her?

How many couples have this problem? Most of them. And if they don't, it is because neither partner ever challenged him or herself, and never changed the belief he or she had when they were first married. This is why a wife can say about her husband, "I know what he likes," and if someone questions, "How do you know that?" the wife will respond, "I have known him for twenty years. I know exactly what he likes. He likes this food, and that and that...." And the husband can say the same about his wife.

Surely if we listen to this kind of testimony, we could be amazed. How can they know each other so well? It is because they never do anything outside of the realm of who they think they are, but only within their character. If we repeat our actions many times, it is understandable that after a while our partner knows what we like and don't like.

But let us say, one spouse starts to take a class in order to learn something new, and meanwhile her partner is watching TV and seeing her come back late every night. He might be happy because at least she is coming back at a specific time. But if one night she comes back and changes her routine according to something she learned from her class, perhaps lighting some candles and meditating, surely her husband will start to question what she is learning, because he sees she is changing. He will start to feel uncomfortable, because due to this minor change he may start to feel that he doesn't know how to relate to her. The thought may pass through his mind, "It took us years to adjust to each other and now she is bringing something new." Is this situation real or not? It is very real.

We are constantly making choices about how we think and act, therefore it is we who create ourselves.

The reason someone reacts to this kind of small change, like lighting a candle, is because the person who watches begins to feel insecure. It can be similar between parents and children. The parents can feel insecure when the children they believe they know start to change. Instead, parents should recognize that children are made to change in order to fulfill their potential. Parents should also acknowledge that if their children were to continue to follow the same behavior for many years, the parents would become worried about them and would push them to expand themselves.

We might question, did God create us to be so insecure and so anchored to our patterns or did we make ourselves this way? One thing is sure: we are constantly making choices about how we think and act, therefore it is we who create ourselves. The problem is, because it takes effort to discover who we can become, we have the tendency to choose a few preferences and some familiar actions.

Our Character is not Ready-Made

When we look at the creation, we could say that its most dramatic characteristic is the amazing variety of animals, plants, and insects living in so many kinds of habitats. Given the complexity of the creation, if we want to fulfill our God-given potential we first must realize that He made us in a way that we can never find out who we are in one day, in one month, in one year, or even over many years.

I think God created Himself in exactly the same way. He created Himself to be able to develop, and for the things He created to be able to develop.

Interestingly, if we look at our external aspect, we can see that we are physically complete: we have two eyes, two ears, one nose, two arms, and so on, all functioning harmoniously. But if we look at our internal character, is it complete?

Regardless it took so many years and so much effort for God to create the majestic animal and plant realms, we human beings who are part of this environment are meant to distinguish ourselves, not just by having a unique external form but by developing a character that surpasses the characters of the plant and animal kingdoms.

If we can accept that our character is not ready-made or static but is something that requires development, then based on this assumption our attitude will change concerning what we think we know, and we will become more open to new things. But developing our character can carry certain consequences as well. For example, have we ever experienced visiting our parents' house after we are grown up and having our mom prepare exactly the same meal that we used to like? Our mom wants to please us by preparing our favorite food, or by keeping the same blanket we used to have in our bedroom, or preserving some of our old games. But regardless we might feel good eating what we used to like, and maybe still like, or finding the same blanket, does our mom really please us? If we have never changed tastes from what we used to like she will still please us, but if we have changed we may feel odd to re-experience these things.

It is similar for friendships. If we meet a friend after a long period of time, at first we will feel happy because we remember the time when we were friends with this person. As all kind of memories come back, our friend may ask us if we remember this event or that. But after a few minutes into the conversation, there may be silence. At that moment, our friend might wonder if we are the same person as before, or we might feel our friend is very similar to when we used to know him. Due to the reality that some persons change and some do not, an uncomfortable situation can occur between old friends.

This is what happened to me when I once returned to my hometown. One man came by and asked, "Do you remember, we played soccer together every day after school? We had such a good time." He tried to communicate with me according to that memory. But I wasn't in the same place, and it was difficult to remember the joy of that event. Due to this kind of thing, we can lose our friendships.

Regardless of this possibility, do you still want to discover yourself? Or, do you just want to remain static with your knowledge of yourself? Actually, we can always know some part of ourselves, because certain aspects manifest themselves in the present time. We know how we react to this and to that, based on our experience. But is this just knowledge about ourselves in the moment, or is this our total life? That is the question. If we never move left nor right, up nor down, we will stay with what we know.

But one thing I can tell you, it is hard to stay the same person throughout the long process of life. If someone believes that keeping the same traditions and behavior is something easy, I will say that the effort to stay the same is as much as it is to change. Therefore, we might as well accept to change and develop. And, if we can evolve our characters through accepting to harmonize with many different situations, sooner or later we will be able to lose our statement of knowing who we are and replace it with, "I remember I used to be that way."

The effort to stay the same is as much as it is to change.

The Danger of Protecting One's Belief

If we consider religious persons, we can see many of them seem to know what they believe, to the point they firmly identify themselves with certain beliefs. Due to this, they really believe they know God's will. But regardless it looks like this unity with their belief gives them strength, if after some years these persons continue to stubbornly uphold their belief as the only one, they will find themselves rejecting many things around them and eventually going backwards in their internal life.

Due to this attitude of wanting to protect one's belief in order to keep one's sense of identity, a religious person might eventually find himself admitting, "I used to experience God. It was wonderful. But you know, these days I don't find God anymore." And the tragedy is, he doesn't know why it happened.

This is a serious situation, isn't it? Shouldn't we worry

about that? We know there were a lot of religious people who dreamed and hoped to become better persons during the course of their lives, but the tragedy is, very few achieved their desire. One of the main reasons their growth stopped was because they began to repeat the phrase, "I know what I believe and what I don't believe."

This kind of statement signals the beginning of stagnation and the eventual descent of a religious person, especially if he rejects others in the name of protecting his absolute belief. He stops evolving; in other words, he stops discovering himself, he stops going where he has never been. Even worse, if he rejects a person who presents an opportunity for him to change and grow, he will take the downhill road.

Because of the popularity of the statement 'I know', we can observe that when a man and a woman become a couple, after awhile they begin to make statements about themselves. Without even being aware they find themselves saying, 'I know who I am,' or "I know who my spouse is" and try to maintain their relationship based on that. But regardless that saying, "I know who I am," appears very stable, the fact is, each person is not as stable as he or she sounds.

Do you understand why? The statement that you know who you are is perhaps true at that particular moment in time, but the inner you, the real you, is always trying to change. When you say you know what you want or you know who you are, it is because you choose one aspect of yourself or one type of behavior, and decide to value this part over other parts.

To build this sense of value, you begin by deciding within your mind who you are, and every time there is a situation that challenges you, your mind will warn you that something is coming to destroy who you are. But, regardless you can make up your mind to protect what you choose to be, the reality is, you will always be wrestling with some situation or with some person because you continue to wrestle with something inside you.

Make Space for New Thoughts

What is the characteristic of a person who opens before life? This kind of person fights against saying, "I know," and instead tries to acknowledge, "I don't know." Basically, this person always allows for the possibility of not knowing something around him; in other words, he opens himself to events that comes his way. That is what we call having an open mind.

In the moment we begin to believe that maybe there is something else we can learn, discover, etc., many things can begin to approach us, like rain can be absorbed by plants that are thirsty. Because life is always in movement and brings us new things, and because human beings are made to give things to each other, there will always be someone who wants to give us something new, physically or mentally.

But when we say, "I know," in this moment we are erecting bars around us. In the beginning these bars are not so thick, but if we keep saying we know for a long time, they will thicken to the point they become impossible to break and eventually we will block everything that tries to approach us. If someone outside us wants to open our mind, he or she will be unable to do so because our mind is already solidified with fixed thoughts.

For example, if I were to visit a Christian congregation and say to them, "God might be different from what you believe," many of them might respond that they know God because they attend Bible classes. And, if I were to ask them if they know God's will, they would answer that they also know that. Believing they know the will of God roots the words 'I know' so strongly in their heads that if we dare to persist in asking how they know, they will usually retort, "I just know."

The question is, do they really know? From the point of view of belief, they can say they know and then the conversation is finished. But from the point of view of life, it is difficult to believe they could know something so completely without giving some room for thought, at least. Based on realizing that life is always moving and changing, this person should say,

People have a tendency to value a position of knowing instead of a position of not being sure.

"I know something already but I welcome new thoughts," or "I don't really know." Surely with this approach toward the will of God they would have a chance to welcome something different from what they know or believe they know. But the fact is, religious people have a tendency to value a position of knowing instead of a position of not being sure, which explains why so many religious persons are more resistant to development, transformation, and new ideas than those who never make a statement of belief.

Indeed, because a religious person puts so much value on knowing the truth, when someone brings a new perspective he will be rejected almost at the speed of light. Due to this reaction, we can understand why it is much more difficult to unite two religious persons or groups than it is to yoke together two horses to pull a carriage.

If we believe it is indeed the religious people who guide the internal direction of a nation, then we should be worried seeing them making the statement they 'know' so often, when maybe they don't know. In a field like science, researchers have a similar difficulty to discover new things if they begin to make the statement that they 'know'—basically it means the end of their research.

When religious persons, in their field of discovering God and their relationship to Him, make so many statements about knowing Him, they start to provoke friction inside themselves and with others instead of harmony. Due to this attitude, they put their souls inside of a prison cell, which I think was not their original goal. Instead, if they could take the road of wanting to discover the way to relate with God, they would create a reputation of being tender and adventurous people, instead of being stubborn and narrow.

Indeed, if religious persons could give some room to accept that they don't know God as they pretend to, they would discover there is a way to find God, and through this discovery they would eventually reach a higher understanding of God. If they were more open, the knowledge they receive would not imprison them, but would instead help them to continue on the road of discovering God.

For ourselves, if we can accept to not make the statement 'I know' too often, this will help us to avoid creating a prison around ourselves. By accepting to review our beliefs, we weaken our bars. And, if an old friend comes close to us again after some years, he or she might remark to us, "You are more accepting of life," meaning that we have been able to accept new aspects of ourselves and of others.

Learn But Let It Go

So, if you have this instinct to make statements, do you now understand the impact upon your character after awhile?

The problem is, usually the first time we make a statement that we 'know' something or that we 'know' who we are, we feel we have made a big accomplishment. But by constantly promoting who we 'are', after a while this character becomes our prison. So many struggles arise in relationships between people because each individual creates his or her own box and the other cannot find a way to open it.

Now we know that to create truly beautiful characters, we must be able to travel everywhere in the journey of life, but never to say 'I know'. We can keep open by affirming, "Maybe there is something else to discover," regardless it is not easy.

When people say, "I know who I am, I know what I like," life, which is in constant motion, gets rejected. Due to this rejection of the events of life, we isolate ourselves to the point that people can view us as being boring or negative.

A common tendency of people is to identify themselves with their culture and their nation. People are

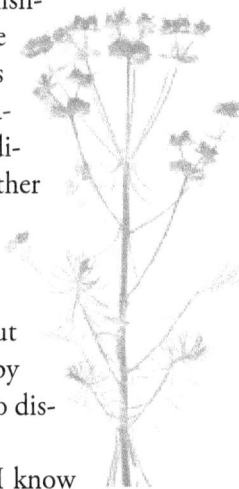

strongly bound to these identities, to the point that friction between them and persons from another culture or country can easily arise. Therefore, it is understandable why God would have a tendency to want to choose young people to do His will, because they don't yet have a strong sense of identity. But this openness usually only lasts for a few years, and after this time has passed, these young persons start to consistently make statements about what they believe.

Knowledge was not made to trap us, rather it was made for us to comprehend and then let it go.

When we consider people who have closed their minds, we can accuse the truth they have learned as being the cause. But the reality is, it is not the truth they believe that is blocking them, it is they who choose to close themselves by creating absolute statements about their beliefs.

So, regardless human beings have the admirable ability to discover new thoughts that can become part of their knowledge, the fact is that when humans reach a certain understanding, they often attach themselves to this understanding and settle there.

But if we look at the purpose of knowledge, we can avow that knowledge was not made to trap us. Rather it was made for us to comprehend and then let it go when we begin to understand, so that we will be able to go to the next stage. Still, regardless we can have the view that it is good to let go of a thought after it has fulfilled its purpose, is it difficult or easy to let it go? It is usually very difficult.

Why is it so hard? It is hard because we want security.

We want to hold on to our beliefs, we want to hold on to our relationships. Perhaps I made a friend at a certain moment of my life when I was beginning my spiritual journey. But let's say my friend changed his beliefs and mine remained the same, then I started to give him a hard time. Why? Because my friend ventured outside of his 'box', the place where we had made a mental or an emotional connection, and where I felt happy and secure. Because this person moved and I did not, after awhile I began to find it difficult to connect with my friend, to the point I maybe even persecuted him for his new beliefs.

Our Inner Self Demands Growth

Regardless nobody wants people to change because they want to be able to remain friends forever, the question is, is it possible to not change? We know that if friends find each other in a mysterious way, they also can lose each other through the process of life. In the case of husband and wife, they especially will not want to discover their spouse has changed. Their wish when they married was to have a relationship that could last at least until the end of their earthly life. But to maintain this unity over a lifetime, each partner has to say to him or herself, "I must not change. If I do, then my spouse will begin to feel distant from me."

Regardless of this vow to resist change, many times when a spouse looks at his or her partner, he or she will discover that something has changed emotionally. This is why many wives say, "I was married with one man, but I don't recognize him anymore." Due to this situation the relationship can deteriorate, to the point it can become icy.

The possibility of changing from one spiritual space to another creates a big problem within the human race. Regardless we dream of keeping the perfect feeling between friends for a long period of time, because humans are made to reach their proper potential, or destiny, it is rare to have stayed the same when we meet an old friend again. But if human beings realize that we are made to develop our spirits and our hearts, we will not be shocked when we find that another human being has changed.

Because the vow of friendship is less strong than a marriage vow, if one friend begins to take the road of changing his spiritual space when the other does not, they can say, "I think we no longer have much in common," and they can just part from each other. But when a wife finds herself in a position where she feels she cannot connect with her husband as she used to, it is much more complex to say to him, "I think it is time to part because we no longer have anything to give to each other, mentally or emotionally."

Is there any hope for these friends or these couples to fulfill their desire to maintain their relationship? To do so, each one will have to vow not to be influenced by anything new, and due to their tenacity in keeping their personality in a box, they can stay together. Another way to maintain their friendship or their marriage throughout the hilly course of life will be for both individuals to accept to change in the same direction, either up or down. Based on taking the same direction, their relationship can maintain itself.

But if one of these friends or spouses develops him or herself for whatever reason, and the other remains the same, this change will destabilize the emotional relationship, and over time the distance between each will become wider and wider. Due to the fact that the internal aspect of humans demands growth, there is always a tendency for human relationships to break apart. But on the other hand, because of this internal demand for development, the human race has the hope of building something greater.

Regardless of why our soul or our inner self asks for growth, this development can only occur if human beings do not proudly remain in their boxes. For example, if we choose to be religious, it should mean we are a person who is constantly looking to develop from one internal space to the next. However, if we do well, we might realize there are fewer people who can meet us in our new space. In other words, if we evolve according to our soul's desire, we may realize that we have no other friends besides the One we have dedicated our lives to, who is God. The best situation will be, regardless of the fulfillment we receive from our personal relationship with God, if we can find someone or some group similar to us with whom we can make friendships.

Because of this internal demand for development, the human race has the hope of building something greater.

Now we know that, due to the possibility of changing from one spiritual sphere to another, there is no guarantee that we will keep the same friends until we are all 60 or 70 years old. Regardless our intention is to be friends forever or married for eternity, we don't know if we are going to finish the journey together or if someone will stop somewhere along the way.

Can We Make Room for God?

If we look at our physical body's development, we realize our body starts with a few cells and hormones and from there it continues to develop almost without our conscious participation, just from giving it physical nourishment.

But if we look at the growth of our soul, we have the freedom to reject its development or to accept to fulfill its desires. In the case of our soul, our participation is much more important than we might realize. It is we who make barriers to growth within our mind by choosing 'I know who I am, I know what I believe,' or by allowing our soul's growth through keeping an open mind.

What we choose mentally will also affect our physical bodies. If we choose to make barriers, we can already feel old at a young age, regardless our body is only 45 or 50 years old. In the land of America, people seem to have more open minds, which means the tendency to make strong statements about who they are is less frequent. But many European people seem to know who they are at a younger age, meaning they get stuck in a specific box much sooner in their journey of life.

Traditionally, most people who came as settlers to America were coming from the land of Europe, and what motivated these native Europeans to go to America is that somewhere in the course of their lives they must have received an inspiration, "I can do something different from my ancestors. " Based on this inspiration, these Europeans tried to break the limitations within themselves and thus were able to make the tumultuous journey to America. It is due to this new cornerstone of thought that American people are able to more easily give up what they believe they know and go wherever God drives them or wherever a new idea can take them.

Regardless that American people have inherited this quality, if they start to make the statement that they 'know,' their destiny at the individual and collective levels will stop short. Although many Americans have the sense that God is with them, if they start to choose the statement 'I know,' then God will abandon them.

Based on the possibility of shifting between wanting to follow God's idea wherever it leads and believing they already know God's plan, it is understandable why religious people could begin to sense that God is not with them and could eventually say that God does not exist or even that He is dead. In other words, regardless how each religious person approaches his or her God, if he or she hears the direction to go somewhere or to do something and answers, "My God, I don't think You know me—I can't do that," it is the end of any positive development in that person's spiritual life.

Due to the fact that many of us stop at a certain level in the development of our soul, we quickly feel old. Each time we repeat the statement 'I know', we block God's love from flowing to our heart, and due to the resulting lack of feeling, our trust in God diminishes.

We have to realize that in the moment we begin to say 'I know what I am doing,' this statement has the power to shut off the connection valve between our mind and our heart, and therefore our soul can no longer receive the spiritual elements it needs for its development. Because we block God from relating with us then God, who generates our evolution, will be obliged to turn His back on us.

This is important if we claim to be a Christian and we often read Jesus Christ's words in the Bible. After a few years of reading our Bible we may start to say, "I know God's will." Then if perchance we receive a revelation from God, it is possible that we will reject this new thought, instead of saying, "God, whatever You want, whatever is next, I will be open. I will go wherever You ask me to go, I will do whatever You ask me to do."

"God, whatever You want, whatever is next, I will be open."

Only by choosing to keep our minds open, can we make room for God to create duality with us. Although we receive inspiration through reading God's word, this inspiration is not meant for us to make a statement of belief, but is meant to help us along the path in order to be able to welcome something more.

If we can keep ourselves from making statements, we have a greater chance of moving up to another level, instead of blocking ourselves and therefore starting to develop resentment, regardless we did not have this intention.

Wisdom Says, "I Don't Know"

If I reflect on my life's path, for many years I proceeded without knowing where I was going. This kind of path is often viewed as strange by others. People tend to ask, "What would you like to do in the future?" and when they hear the answer, "I don't know, I will see," they question, "You don't know where you are going?"

From their questioning we might perceive that they have planned everything about their own future, yet over time most people will begin to realize they don't really know what will happen, as they discover they are not in control of every aspect of life.

Regardless we might encounter this kind of question about our future from people of all different ages, the wise way to perceive life is not, "I know who I am, I know what I want," but instead, "I don't know who I am and I don't know where I am going," However, if we give this kind of response, we have to realize that people might persecute us for not having any personality.

The reason I speak about avoiding a statement of belief is because when we observe religious people, one of their common attributes is that they have come to a point where they make the statement that they 'know.' Due to this, every religious person gets stuck at a certain place, which may eventually become a name, like "The Church of …" Basically, their beliefs become a church or a denomination that they identify with.

However, if we look at life as a road we have to take in order to become one with the heart of God, the instinct of our soul will be to demand that we keep moving until we finish at the bosom of God.

On the other hand, if religious people begin to identify themselves with 'I know,' then it is understandable why certain pockets will be formed, to the point they could obtain a name like Catholic or Protestant, Episcopalian, Baptist or Presbyterian. Forming a denomination makes religious people feel secure about their beliefs. Even people who believe in nothing specific often say, "I know who I am and what I like," because saying these words gives them a sense of security.

If religious people resist making the statement "I know" in regards to what they believe, it means they have chosen to have faith in what they discover. What a faith is needed in order to go where tomorrow leads, regardless we don't know what tomorrow has in store for us!

The instinct of our soul demands that we keep moving until we finish at the bosom of God.

If faith in God is difficult, faith in relationships between human beings is even more demanding, mainly because we never know what people will do in various situations. Dealing with material things is much more secure: I have my job, my things, I know exactly where my house is, what kinds of clothes I like to wear. However, in relationships we receive no guarantee of where we are going, basically because we don't know where people will be the next day, physically, mentally, or spiritually. Why is it so complicated? Because people are always changing their thoughts and actions.

If people could behave like our furniture, surely the quantity of faith we would need to have in them would be much less. This is the reason, if we attend a family gathering or a school reunion, we hope to find people exactly the same as they were when we previously knew them. As well, we like our friends or our partner to remain constant. However, because our inner being demands us to increase in understanding and love, people are constantly moving and changing.

When we first meet someone, we may feel something for that person, and due to this we may accept to engage ourselves as a partner with him or her. But we need to keep in mind from the very beginning of the relationship, did we meet each other for a journey together or did we meet each other to be stuck in one place together?

In many cases, one of the partners moves to a different mental or spiritual place, while the other chooses to stay in the same place. Due to this discrepancy, it is understandable why sooner or later the relationship will become strained or even break down. Sometimes, due to the desire to keep a relationship intact, one partner will bow down and say, "Do whatever you like, and I will go with you."

If we have confidence that we are going in the direction of God's love, then it is wonderful if our partner can have faith in us, because he or she can move with us as we progress to each new realm. Through this faith, if on our pathway we have the honor to discover God, our partner will be able to do so as well.

Trust What is Outside of Yourself

When people choose to stay in one place because they believe it is too stressful to move, they should be aware that anyone who doesn't move forward will feel stressed anyway, because he will find himself slowly declining. If we don't want to find ourselves stagnating somewhere we need to go forward, and then we won't be stressed, because we will have discovered more space within our being.

This is similar to the situation of a child who wants to stay in bed. His mom may say, "Come on, get out of bed," and he responds, "I can't." His mom might continue, "I know you can't, that is why I will stand here until you move!" Then when he gets up he will receive energy, because he will be seeing from the perspective of standing up.

Basically, education is about presenting something new to a person. Regardless this person's first thought could be, "I cannot believe that, it is too much," if he can just accept to listen with openness, he will hear inside himself, "Trust what you hear." He might object, "Trust what?" And the response could come, "Trust what is outside of yourself."

Anyone who doesn't move forward will feel stressed, because he will find himself slowly declining.

Regardless what someone outside could suggest, if that person still prefers to choose what he feels inside, he will insist, "I couldn't succeed yesterday, so it will be the same today." But the one outside will maybe reply, "Yesterday was yesterday, and today is another day. How do you know the same thing will happen again?"

All we know is what happened the first time we tried something new, but we don't know what will happen the second time. It is possible that we will fail again, but the third time will be another opportunity. Even after ten times, we need to stand up again.

Do you understand why God doesn't have anyone in the world who can do His will? It is because we know we will experience stress and difficulty when we try to do something that stretches our concepts. Due to this perception, we create the thought that we are not qualified to fulfill God's desire.

Somebody once asked me, "Why does God ask us to do something when we are not prepared to do it?" It is a good question, isn't it? Why doesn't He ask somebody else? Why us and not that other person who looks more qualified to do what God wants?

Basically, if we listen to our thoughts, we could believe we are not made to challenge ourselves. But if we look around us, we realize that many people challenge others, like all the teachers who stand up in front of their students. Basically, these teachers ask the students to walk where they don't feel like walking. In order to go somewhere new, we need to learn new subject matter, and as well we have to accept to trust the person who presents this material. But often we are looking at our feet instead of looking toward where we are going!

We tend to want to use our knowledge to make us feel more secure. But today I have said that what we already know is not our total destiny. Therefore we cannot make the decisive statement that we know who we are.

One thing we always have to keep in mind is that in order to go from one stage to the next one, we need to proceed by faith, and in order to go to the next stage, we need to go by faith again. That is why whenever we go to someplace new, it is always hard because it requires some part technique and some part faith.

So, what should we do with what we already know? We might become a teacher of others who want to gain new knowledge, or perhaps we can glorify ourselves that we somehow made it this far. But regardless we have grown our knowledge, we should question ourselves, is it enough to reach the finish line?

Should we feel miserable about this situation? Remember, a doctor doesn't make us ill by telling us that we are sick and we need to take a different road, so don't kill the doctor. Remember, the doctor only tells us our status, but this isn't what makes us sick.

If a prophet comes to tell us that we are incomplete or that we still have sin, we should not reject him because of our tendency to believe it is he who creates our problem. Many people say to the prophet, "If you didn't tell me I have sin, I wouldn't know. Therefore I wouldn't feel that I am sinful." But the truth is, prior to the arrival of the prophet, we already feel that something isn't going well, and the prophet just comes to help us to clarify our situation and to know what direction to take.

Faith and Obedience

When we are called by God to take the journey to follow our soul, in the beginning it might feel easy, because since we don't know much, God doesn't ask us so much at first. After some time, however, it is more difficult to do God's will because He begins to ask things related to our specific level, and we start to recall what we already know. But by recalling our previous knowledge we create a cage that blocks us from staying open in front of the demands of God. Due to this it becomes difficult for God to ask something new from us, and therefore our progress stops. This is why very few human beings can arrive at the place where we can claim to be free from our historical disease of sin.

In a business, if one of the workers quits it means the boss must find someone else to do the job. Regardless that a worker who accepts a job says at first that he will be loyal to his new boss, after some years this same worker may find himself in the position of rebelling against the boss or looking for a new job. The reason people can behave this way is because they begin to measure everything they have been through, and they don't want to continue to keep giving all of their effort.

Regardless it may be true that we have been through many things, when we begin to say 'I already know' we don't just create a box, but we put ourselves on top of a mountain, as well. Basically, every time we say, 'I know,' it means we think we are the boss, and no one can tell us anything.

When a person's faith and desire to move step-by-step toward his divine destiny are contaminated by the thought 'I know', he will be stopped in his tracks.

If we decide to take the road to reach the divinity of God's love, we will need to trust and to obey the demands that present themselves along the way.

Maybe we have heard of the story of Peter walking on the water. At first, Jesus said to Peter, "Come to me." Although Peter started out with his eyes upon Jesus, he faltered when he diverted his gaze towards the water and the wind. If Peter had kept looking at Jesus with trust, surely he could have stayed on top of the water. But perhaps because Peter knew he could not swim, he said to himself, "I know I can't swim, therefore I am really stupid to be trying this."

Regardless this might be a symbolic story, the message can be for our daily life. When we need to go somewhere, where are we looking? Are we looking inside of us at what we already know, or are we looking outside of us and saying, "I will walk there even though I don't know where I am going"?

The story of Peter is vivid because it illustrates two

directions: one that represents what the Lord opens to us and the other that looks inside of us. We hear the call outside of us to walk toward some unfamiliar situation, while another voice inside of us says, "I cannot." Due to these two distinct voices, we have to make the same kind of choice Peter was confronted with. Based on whether we choose to believe we know or to be open to an adventure, we create our soul's destiny.

The story of Peter describes his private choice: doubting and therefore being submerged by the water, which represented his sin, or going beyond the doubts of his flesh, which would permit him to go where Jesus asked him, represented as Peter walking on the water. If today we still struggle between these two major choices, it means we stand where Peter did and many others as well.

Regardless it is a wonderful idea to want to follow Jesus as our Lord, the real dilemma will be when he asks us to do something that sounds as crazy as Peter walking on top of the water. When someone asks us to do something we've never done before, it might feel like we are going to our death. Due to our fear, it is easier to retreat toward something we already know about.

Freedom to Relate With God

We have to always be careful to welcome new experiences, because how do we know what process the God of the Universe will use to lead us to our divine destiny?

Many times He will bring us a person with a new idea, hoping that we will choose this new view instead of blocking ourselves by throwing the words 'I know' at this person. To avoid blocking the way, we need to choose the best attitude, which is the understanding that God will use people to educate us. Then we will begin to experience a miracle: the cage we have formed around our soul by so often stating 'I know" will be weakened.

God will keep sending us different situations in hope we will choose the road we don't know, instead of choosing to stagnate in a place that in the long term would be regrettable. We have to keep the awareness that if a new friend appears, or a new job situation arises, we will be able to change and grow only if we do not pronounce the words 'I know' before this new event has a chance to unfold.

When religious people do not want to welcome a new situation, they will often say, "This cannot be the desire of God," which permits them to attack or reject a new event. People who don't identify themselves as religious may just say, "I am not good at this kind of activity." Regardless whether we identify ourselves as religious or not, in the moment we choose to not make the statement "I don't think I can do this" or "I don't think I will like this" and choose instead to keep our minds open, we can be directed to a place where limitations can be overcome and barriers becomes less inhibiting.

If our objective is vast, it is normal that God will never cease to send us different events in order to help us to break every wall or box we ever created. As we welcome many events, our souls will become free to develop a relationship with God, which, simply expressed, will develop our character of goodness.

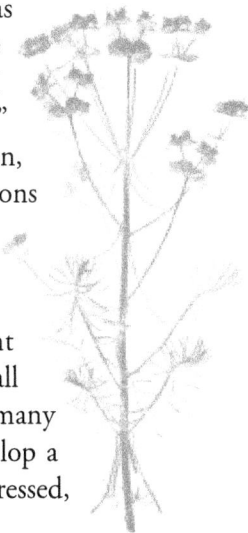

So, if we want to create a relationship with God, we must flow with the events that present themselves to us. Prayer will only help us if we pray to welcome the events of life. In other words, to develop a relationship with God we must always be expanding our personality by keeping our minds open.

Prayer will only help us if we pray to welcome the events of life.

Regardless we know that between people it is usually through words that a relationship starts, whether we are able to stay together depends on what soul we have, or what dimension of personality we have. If a couple chooses to move forward on the same road of welcoming new events, they will be able to develop the same dimension of soul.

So, what causes struggles in relationships between friends and couples? Did only one individual take the road toward achieving divinity or did both of them move in that direction? Did one accept to change while the other one refused to go forward? Due to this reality, which is often not so visible, people experience massive frustration and misunderstandings with each other.

This difference in attitudes is why it is so hard to solve problems in relationships. Regardless in the beginning we may try to help our friend or our partner, starting off with plenty of desire and making lots of effort, we may realize the other person cannot move. Although everyone believes they can help each other, the reality is that the one who grows will find it difficult to live with the gap that he or she has created, and may end up in despair, as well as the one who didn't grow.

Love is Our Destiny

If humans want to come out from their boxes, they have to give up something they think they know. For example, some people may say, "I am not made to be religious." This means that they believe they are something else. And because they insist on believing they are not religious, they can never be religious today, tomorrow, or ever. If another person says, "I am not a businessman," that means he believes he is something else, and he will never be able to become a businessman. And, if a businessman says, "I cannot be a husband, I am not good at that," it is because he believes that he is only meant to be a businessman, not a husband.

Due to our beliefs, we have so few relationships in our lives, and many of them are weak and fragile. And, if we do have a relationship, if one person moves to a different space it looks like all of a sudden we no longer have a relationship. Because there are a multitude of persons in the world, regardless we can lose one friend, we might still feel that we can find someone else who is at the same place where we are. However, because the relationship between couples is unique and is meant to last a long time, they both need to be careful to not make the statement 'I know' before experiencing new events, in order for both to grow and therefore to be able to stay together.

So, if we choose to welcome life, which means to welcome new situations, we must educate ourselves to say, "I don't know where this situation will lead me, but I will find out." What if God asks us to welcome ten people into our home? At first we would probably respond, "I cannot handle that." And yes, it is true that the way we currently are, we cannot stand the idea of having ten people stay in our house. Well, at least we are sincere. We know our character very well. So, what has to happen? Should we reject all these people? One thing is sure, if nobody comes, we will stay as we are, enjoying our peace and quiet, happy to not be disturbed. But since God knows we are building a stronger cage every day by rejecting what comes to us, He doesn't want to leave us there.

If our purpose were not to create and to experience love, it would be okay to leave each individual inside his or her box, but when we know that love is our destiny, it is difficult to allow someone to create a sarcophagus, just as this person is beginning his or her life journey. But because most people don't know much about how love functions in reality, they often accept another way of 'loving', which is to allow others to create their boxes, in the name of not bothering them.

If people could only realize that when they hold on strongly to what they believe, they will end up rejecting many new events. If instead they can be open, they will grow themselves because every new experience can become a part of them.

Digest Events and Grow Our Heart

The process of digesting what life offers to us is similar to how our body's bloodstream functions. Our white blood cells are made to engulf and digest what does not belong inside us, like certain bacteria. Let's say, tomorrow our white cells refuse to fight the bacteria, saying to us, "You know, I can no longer digest these disgusting bacteria."

And we might respond to them, "Why not?"

And the white blood cells might answer, "I just cannot do it."

What shall we do then? If our cells refuse to fulfill this task, we will be obliged to find some machine that can clean our blood. But the question still remains, what is going to happen to us, who carry these reluctant cells? Are we going to become weaker or stronger?

The more our cells find the way to defend our bodies by devouring invasive bacteria, the more we become strong. So figuratively we can say, the more we digest the 'bacteria' of life, the more we become strong.

When we hold on too strongly to our beliefs, we find ourselves rejecting anything that is unfamiliar.

Therefore we should question, what do we want to become? If we don't want to grow, then we will try to run away from the 'bacteria', or pass them onto someone else. But I will say something: if we cannot digest what life presents to us, it is similar to trying to escape from all bacteria. In the end we will become sick, because our body did not create antibodies and therefore cannot give us any protection when a worst-case situation arises.

If we find ourselves underdeveloped, it is basically because we rejected over and over what life offered to us, regardless that some of those events were negative and we could easily feel justified in rejecting them. However, if we remove the 'I know who I am' or 'I know what I can do,' we will change the direction of our focus from being self-centered to making ourselves centered outside ourselves, and even negative events can be accepted and digested. If we choose to be centered on what life can offer to us, instead of feeling fearful, God can begin to give us many situations that will allow us to develop ourselves.

If we compare encountering new situations or new people to being exposed to new bacteria, we might realize that in order to make us strong we need to receive more and more challenges. We therefore must not try to stay in a place where we are insulated from everything.

The reason God gives us all these 'bacteria' or people is because He wants us to be able to receive Him someday. God is big. Maybe He represents twelve kinds of 'bacteria', or even twelve thousand kinds of 'bacteria'. Therefore, if we can learn to digest twelve or twelve thousand kinds of 'bacteria', it means one day we can have a heart similar in size to God's Heart.

The point I want to address is, because we don't know how big God is, we should want to expand ourselves as much as possible in order to harmonize with Him one day. Therefore, we surely have to learn to digest all that He wants us to digest.

When we look at the characteristics of human beings, we can say there are maybe twelve major characteristics, sometimes represented as the twelve gates of heaven, which means God as the Creator must have, as well, twelve major characteristics. Therefore, if our objective is to be able to love God or to become part of God, the only way is to accept all these kinds of characteristics, because doing so enables us to become big and wide enough to approach God Himself.

When we accept what God gives to us, it is like we are able to 'consume' God. Perhaps what I say looks implausible, but consider that when we consume food, something develops inside our body.

Those who feel they can live anywhere, on any continent, with any kind of people, can begin to be able to approach God.

Some people feel that they can only relate with their family and relatives, or only with their ethnic group, race or nationality. But others feel they can make friends from many races, nations and continents. Which kind of people are closest to God? Those who feel they can live anywhere, on any continent, with any kind of people, can begin to be able to approach God—doesn't that make sense?

Let's say we can learn to digest three kinds of 'bacteria' or three types of characters or three people from different continents, then can we understand why God will challenge us to digest three more? Every time we are able to digest an event that normally might cause us to feel discomfort or resentment, God can approach us and begin to give some of His heart. But if we choose to say, "I think I cannot do that," then we will start to lose the benefit of having already digested three kinds of people. Due to this internal secret, when we refuse to digest something new, it is similar to being deprived of physical nourishment.

Based on this law of either going forward or going backward, many good people who have been able to digest quite a few difficult situations start to decline after awhile. In fact, if we listen to our thoughts, we will realize that after digesting only a few events we often begin to say, "I am tired, it is not worth it," or "I just cannot accept this anymore."

We need to keep in mind that it is God who presents new situations to us. Therefore, as potential children of God, instead of wrestling with what God gives to us, let's just wrestle against our tendency to reject. Find a way to accept. Don't find a way to pass on the difficulty to somebody else, because through this we weaken ourselves, to the point we can destroy our inner selves. This is why each situation has to be viewed as a chance for us to grow, regardless that some situations look like they will destroy us.

In contrast to our perception, what actually destroys us is when we don't want to move forward into a situation that is presented to us, but choose instead to retreat inside ourselves. Constant preoccupation with ourselves, or self-centeredness, will bring us to depression. Instead, happy is the one who is in front of God and says, "I don't know." It means that every time this person encounters a situation, he chooses, "Let's see how to proceed in this situation."

To protect ourselves from making the statement "I know", we should not dwell on the past. Instead, it is better to believe that we can digest whatever arises because we have already been able to digest many things. Regardless we might think we already know what will happen, the reality is that every experience can be different from what happened in the past. Therefore, we have to keep our minds open. Through acceptance, we will develop a larger personality as a result, which will help us to digest even more situations.

Come Before God as a Child

Whether our character represents the east or the west, the north or the south, what makes our real personality is how much we have digested or rejected things. When we were young, maybe it was difficult to digest our own brothers and sisters. But if we learned to live with them, we will now say it is a piece of cake to be close to them, even though we may still find it difficult to digest other people who do not come from our direct family.

Happy is the one who is in front of God and says, "I don't know."

Many times life will ask us not only to welcome people who come from our family, our hometown, or our native country, but to digest people from other countries as well. By accepting these challenges we will be able to like not just a few people, but their entire cultures or countries through them.

This means that just a few people can represent the size of the world. The struggle to learn to accept all of their characteristics will make us bigger than we can imagine, eventually becoming big enough to actually fit the whole world inside of us. This is very hopeful!

Through the process of creating a bigger personality, the people around us can begin to perceive love emanating from us. The reason is, as we are able to accept more characteristics in people, especially if they represent different cultures or countries, we can begin to meet God's heart.

If we choose the road of discovering ourselves instead of believing we know, God will bring us people in order to move us forward on this road to divinity. If we choose to humble ourselves before the God of heart, He will give us love that will make us bigger. But if we reject the idea of transforming ourselves into bigger people, we will always reject those we struggle with, and we will justify our struggle by saying we already know what will happen. Due to this, the step we take will be backwards.

If we have a religious background, we may be familiar with a song with the lyrics, "I want to walk as a child…." This means, not knowing. It is just like Jesus said: "Truly I tell you, anyone who will not receive the kingdom of God like a little child will never enter it." (Lk 18:17)

As we are able to accept more characteristics in people, we can begin to meet God's heart.

A child doesn't know anything before arriving at a situation. We therefore say that a child is innocent. We are adults, but we must have an innocent heart. The more we challenge our character to go from smaller to bigger, the more we will become, slowly by slowly, like a little child who is just discovering what is going on.

Maybe God wants to talk to us through someone. However, in order for God to be able to speak through someone, that person must have the attitude of discovering and must not act as if he knows. If we, as well, want to recognize the voice of God, we will need to have the attitude to focus on God and not on who God's voice speaks through.

Due to our long lifespan on this Earth, the tendency of people who know a lot is to act upon what they know and to forget to erase, as they proceed, the road of their life. Then when God asks something new of them, they cannot accept it.

There is nothing wrong in acting upon what we know, but when God asks some new challenge, instead of welcoming it, we may choose to glorify what we have already passed through. When God asks us to move on to something new, it is difficult because our experiences come back to us. Based on this reality, we can even say it is more difficult to give up what we know than to give up what we own.

Interestingly, when we find a person who has difficulty to remember events, this person also has a tendency to not make the statement 'I know.' Due to this person's attitude, we may find it easier to speak to him or to her than to someone who remembers everything and always interrupts us by saying, "I know."

So, what about us? Personally, I know what I have been through, but I do not know what the next event will be. To keep this attitude, we need to say, "I know what You made me pass through, Heavenly Father, but I don't know where You will lead me next." There is no self-centeredness in this sentence. It means that I am just with God and grateful to be with Him, and whatever He asks me to pass through I will accept. In this sentence we can recognize there is God first, and then maybe us eventually.

Humble Ourselves in Front of God

Why is it such a big mistake to assert 'I know'? The reason this statement is so powerful is because it allows us to present ourselves as equal to or above someone else. If we start to say "I know" to God, it means we put ourselves equal to God, and if we insist that we know over a long period of time, we will put ourselves above God.

To reverse the position of being equal to or above God, the best way is to begin to trust the life that God brings to us—basically to accept new situations.

Perhaps we are on a trip and discover that our suitcase has disappeared, our suitcase that has all our important things in it. If we have learned to accept all situations that come to us, afterward our suitcase for some reason can come back. We don't really know who took it away or who brought it back. It is a mystery. Regardless this kind of situation can occur because human beings misplace things, the best thing we can do is to be grateful that things that disappear can come back.

If we accept the events of our daily lives, we will develop beautiful personalities, because we will have innocent minds like little children. Surely if God sees us with this kind of mind, He will be pulled to us. If we can humble ourselves before God by saying, "My God, can You help me to accept?" then God will be pleased to come to give His wisdom and love. But if we come before Him with the thought, "I don't like what is being asked of me," God cannot come close to us.

If we face difficulty to accept some situation, yet can accept to humble ourselves before our God, He will bestow upon us a feeling that will allow us to digest the situation. But if we lose that attitude of humility, we will discover that every difficulty will increase, to the point it will feel like the only way to protect ourselves from the worst will be to reject the situation.

Basically, God wishes to be able to see us arrive at a

place where His love can reach us anytime and anywhere. Due to this desire, God will be obliged to ask us to accept many situations throughout our physical lives. But to accept these situations, we will need Him. Otherwise, we will start to reject everything, and feel we have the right to complain. Have we gone to God and asked, "God, how can I change my friend?" or asked ourselves, "Why doesn't she change?"

If we accept the events of our daily lives, we will have innocent minds like little children.

So, what kind of heart do we need to have before God? God likes to hear us begging Him, in order for Him to make a miracle, with our participation. Basically, God knows that it is impossible for us alone to change ourselves or others. He also knows that He cannot change everything by Himself. Basically, no matter how big God's contribution is, if a human does not find some kind of desire within to become divine, this individual will not arrive at his or her heart's desire.

Do Everything With God

So, if we don't want to block our way by saying, "I know," it means we must take the road of an open mind in order to bring God in our midst. If our desire is to become godly, we need God—we cannot become holy without God's presence. Throughout history many Christians had the desire to build the Kingdom of Heaven, but eventually may have questioned, did they build the Kingdom of Heaven or did they build a kingdom where they forgot God?

Indeed, regardless people hear the voice of their soul that wishes to become one with God, if an individual does not welcome God throughout his day, everyday, this person will not arrive where he was hoping. Based on this, God knows that unless humans choose to welcome His contribution each day, these humans will stop on their journey and will begin to believe they know.

If we observe what people want, we realize they want to change the world. It is a heavy-duty job. Therefore it is understandable that if we want to make this world good, we need God. If our dream is to create a great place, our first requirement is to always stay with God. If we can maintain this first step, which is the unity between us and our God, then when we begin to feel the weight, we will be able to digest it.

Because the world is so big, we have to accept to do things with God, and with the help of God we will begin to perceive that the world is not too big. But if we choose to try to achieve things by ourselves, we will be leveled by the weight of the world.

If we walk with Him throughout our lives, we can win something incredible, which is to win His heart. Even if we don't gain any secular results, we can still win the heart of God. If this can happen by the end of our physical life, surely God will welcome us in His place of divinity.

Based on this reality, it is wise to not wait until we are near to the end of our lives to desire to be with God, because it is possible that we will encounter too large of an obstacle. Instead, if from today we choose the road to reverse the 'I know who I am' by accepting to discover ourselves, we will realize we can easily find people in our lives who have different characteristics that we need to learn to like. Through this, we will gain wisdom and find that as we learn to digest people, we can eventually meet God who is the Origin of all characteristics.

If we walk with God throughout our lives, we can win something incredible, which is to win His heart.

'To digest' means to accept to live with people. If we take this road, we can say we have great hope, because based on this honorable road, we will be able to meet the God of Heaven.

What is amazing about the road of discovering ourselves is that God is watching how we will find Him in the process of our physical lives. He watches everybody, nobody more, nobody less. There are no elite. In His eyes, there is only the person who becomes His image or not.

To achieve this call of our soul, we need to digest the 'bacteria' He gives to us. The more we perform this miracle, the more we will be viewed as a good person. Therefore, the definition of good people is those who have the desire and take the pathway to make room for God.

Based on this extraordinary destiny, we need to say, "I have the conviction in the midst of my life to digest whatever comes my way, because through this effort, I will be able to receive the gift of finding God." Due to our incredible achievement as an individual, we will have no difficulty in keeping loyal friends. And if these friends also accept to walk along the road to find God, surely together we will be able to experience joy and love. This is the mystery and the beauty of this road.

Regardless humans have the power to choose whatever they wish, if they want to be good they will need to take the same road in order to become as large as God. As well, since it is us who decide whether or not to digest life, and not God, our choice will not only take us on different roads—the road of goodness or the road of rejection—but it will make God valuable or useless, as well.

If we consider we are victims, then based on the law of duality we have to remember that we are not alone: God will also be a victim. But if we choose to accept life and to discover every part of it in a positive way, our destiny will be joyful, and God, whom we have invited through the process, can also be joyful.

According to the potential of the human race, it is clear that if we make our journey of life based on 'I know', we will condemn ourselves before we can discover our full destiny. To reverse this predestination of limiting our potential, why not allow events to come to us and transform them in wisdom and love with God, since this will allow us to reach the place where God dwells?

Based on these two major opposing roads, I hope your wisdom will be to follow your soul that wishes to accept all things, instead of following your physical instincts that want to reject what comes to you.

May your destiny be to find the space where God dwells inside you.

Thank you, and God bless you.

www.ingramcontent.com/pod-product-compliance
Lightning Source LLC
Chambersburg PA
CBHW071643040426
42452CB00009B/1750